SUCCESS TIPS FOR THE
YOUNG, FLY AND FOOLISH

Table of Contents

THE VISION 10
FILTERING OUT THE FOG 16
THERE'S NO EXCUSE FOR EXCUSES 21
TIMING IS EVERYTHING 25
AVERAGE IS BORING 29
TURN LEMONS INTO LEMON MERINGUE PIE 33
LOVE WHAT YOU DO, AND DO WHAT YOU LOVE ... 37
FEAR IS FICTIONAL 40
BELIEVE IN YOURSELF 43

We are Walking on Air

We are the free spirits that live and walk above the stereotypes and negativity that consumes the universe. The individuals who walk on air are free and willing to take a leap of faith and live in the clouds. The clouds represent a place of serenity where dreamers can dream and creative minds are free to construct the unfathomable. We realize that every day is a gift from God and every moment should be celebrated through smiles, laughter and freedom.

Introduction

For the

Young *dreamers that are*

Fly *enough to soar above all negativity and*

Foolish *enough to believe that they can accomplish what the majority deem impossible or unimaginable*

It took John a while to realize that something was wrong. It was 6:30 a.m, and he was already in the office for a meeting. He looked around at his coworkers and saw a couple of them still wiping the cold from their eyes. One guy put his head down on the desk. The others started to trickle in a little after the scheduled time. The manager saw them walk in late, and made a note on his clipboard, writing them up for tardiness. John worked for a data-processing company that required a high level of proficiency and accuracy from every worker. All of the workers' performances and activities were recorded and measured daily. John's manager stood up, cleared his throat, and began the meeting. He began by going over the rules and setting expectations for the month.

"If you all follow the rules and do what I tell you, then one day, if you're worthy, you may see yourself in my shoes," the manager said with confidence.

The manager's statement didn't sit well with John. John looked around at his co-workers to see if the statement had had the same effect on them, but apparently it hadn't. He knew something was wrong. "Be in his shoes?" John thought, frowning, as he shook his head in confusion. There was nothing appealing about the manager or his duties, nothing at all. Why would John want to work his butt off to be in *his* shoes? John felt as if he was capable of more.

He didn't feel as if he was better than the manager, but John did know that he had so much more to offer to the world. His imagination was too vast, his dreams were too big, and his ambition was unmatched. Additionally, to think that the manager controlled John's destiny was scary. The manager and leadership team monitored his hours and determined his salary, workload, and promotions, all of which troubled John. It could take him years to prove to his superiors that he was worthy of an advancement, and that was still contingent on the managers not firing him before then.

That's when he knew: he was a rebel. That's when he figured out that he couldn't let his destiny be in the hands of another individual. That's when he realized that he wanted to create, build, inspire, and do the things he could only dream of, without compromise. Why? Because the thought of living a mediocre life not in alignment with his goals and dreams was depressing. He'd watched so many other individuals live such mundane lives. It was as if they had died a long time ago. They weren't physically dead, but their dreams had perished, which turned them into nothing more than walking zombies. Their lives were unfulfilling because they chose to settle for a position or job that they knew would deprive them of their ability to pursue their true passion. They lived each day without zeal, passion, or purpose. They let their circumstances suck the life right out of them. From that moment forward, John was a different man.

Everyday someone clocks into work and consults—and copes—with colleagues who have given up on and become content with their lives while complaining about finances, being overworked, and stressing over job security. The problem is that they've mentally adapted to their current situation, a situation which has become just OK for them. Many are afraid to even dream of new beginnings. They prefer not to cloud their minds with such possibilities; instead they create excuses and doubt.

Escaping this box of contentment starts in the mind. We have to personally confirm our dreams and goals and be confident in knowing that every single one of them is attainable. We believe that many of our readers feel the same way. Maybe they are working in a temporary job and living an unfulfilling life, but they desire more! This book is for those people. Am I describing you?

May these tips guide you and serve as a beacon of light as you venture into your uncharted expedition. If nothing else, we hope that they motivate you to chase your dreams and settle for nothing less than all of what you pray for.

These tips were designed to serve as a resource for you during your journey towards success, as reminders to the faint-hearted that anything and everything is possible. We can all learn from others and capitalize on our failures during this journey. Staying focused, motivated, and persistent can become a constant battle, and it is easy for our goals and ambitions to get lost among the negativity and barriers the world presents us. The box that society tries to place us in is persistent in its efforts and only few have the desire and will to escape it. This book is for the individual that doesn't want to be marginalized to conform and to fit into society's pre-made boxes. This book is for those who yearn to live their wildest dreams without compromise. These foolish few have the potential to create their destinies, control their paths, and live their lives in the clouds, full of satisfaction and pleasure. **The time is now!**

Tip #1 The Vision

"The only thing worse than being blind, is having sight but no vision." - Helen Keller

"The best way to predict the future is to create it." - Alan Kay

Who do you want to be 10 years from now? Who do you want to be 20 years from now? Not sure? Imagine who the ultimate version of yourself would be. Back in the introduction, John knew that working at the data processing company for the rest of his life was not a goal of his. John's ultimate version of himself was to be a successful movie producer. John was aware that if he had stayed at the data processing company and continued to try to prove to his manager that he was worthy of a promotion, his conscience would eat him up inside. Burying his ideas, his passion, and his vision for becoming a movie producer was painful. John couldn't live his whole life in regret, wondering what would've happened if he had pursued his dream.

How about you?

If you had absolutely no fears that stopped you from pursuing that dream, who would you become? What skills would you have? What businesses or organizations would you be a part of? Who would you know personally? How much money would you have? Isn't it exciting to think about those possibilities? Whatever person you envisioned, that's actually who you are! That is the person that God wants you to be, the ultimate version of yourself. But before you can even imagine what achieving success feels like, you must envision it. You have to *live* it even before you know how you are going to get there. The saying is true: prior planning prevents poor performance and falling short of your goals. Being thorough and mapping out your goals in a strategic format will be important. In order to make progress you must have a plan of specific actions that you will take to fulfill your life's mission. That's why our first tip to you is to think about your vision, and to create it.

They who have no central purpose in their life fall an easy prey to petty worries, fears, troubles, and self-pitying, all of which are indications of weakness, which lead, just as surely as deliberately planned sins (though by a different route), to failure, unhappiness, and loss, for weakness cannot persist in a power evolving universe. - James Allen, As a Man Thinketh

This quote by James Allen helps us explain why your vision is vital in your journey to success.

The process that it takes to construct a vision will eventually aid you in finding your purpose, for all those who live a meaningful life possess the passion and commitment needed to succeed. We all know someone who works just to work, spending more time living out others' purposes and not their own, which consequently leads them to feel miserable at their jobs. James Allen urges us to find our own purpose. We couldn't agree more. Save yourself from living a meaningless life and take as much time as you need to align yourself with God's purpose for you and your talents.

Creating Your Vision

You can find a million and one ways to properly create your vision, but we believe that your vision is nothing more than a compilation of all your dreams, goals, and aspirations, all in one place, all visible and easily accessible. Anything that you need, want or desire should be here, and we urge you to be as unrealistic as possible. Think of your vision as not what could be, but will be. Essentially, you are using this tool to *create* your own destiny. The chances of you stumbling into success by accident are slim to none, but a clear vision will lead the way. Dreams and passions without strategy are nothing more than fantasies. Keeping these thoughts trapped in your mind cannot be a substitute for having those thoughts displayed in something tangible.

Let us be clear in saying that there are no stipulations or barriers to how you construct your visions. You can use a vision board, pen and paper, a computer, paint and canvass, tape recorder, or anything else. You can get images from magazines, newspapers, books, or whatever source that is available to you. Let your creativity and personality flow freely and decide the direction. Additionally, writing out your personal strategic vision can be very helpful. This usually includes detailed goals, both short term and long term. This can be done by writing your goals in a listed format, or by writing your vision in paragraph format. No matter what route you choose, you must pull your visions from your mind and lay them all out. The platform you choose should completely embody the lifestyle that you want to live. Every detail counts, from the make and model of the car of your dreams to the position and company that you will have. Be sure your vision is something you can edit, and update on a daily basis. You should look at your vision every day to remind yourself who you are, who you plan to be, and where you plan to go. Your vision will be the force that pulls you toward success and keeps you focused along the journey—because we can assure you that it will be a journey full of distractions and obstacles.

Tip #2 Filtering Out the Fog

"That's my gift. I let that negativity roll off me like water off a duck's back. If it's not positive, I didn't hear it. If you can overcome that, fights are easy." - George Foreman

"To all the other dreamers out there, don't ever stop or let the world's negativity disenchant you or your spirit. If you surround yourself with love and the right people, anything is possible." - Adam Green

Stay focused, confident, and filter out the fog. Your vision, interests, and talents weren't given to you by accident. God gave them to you for a reason. So what are some things that we let hinder us from reaching our goal of being all that we can be? There are two things in particular: our surroundings, and ourselves. Most of the time, our surroundings (other people, media, etc.) fog our minds with enough negativity and irrelevant information to block our vision. There is information thrown at us constantly, from news updates, to social media, to apps on our phones, to friendly gossip—the list goes on and on. All of this information can sometimes make us forget our true intentions on earth, so we sometimes just start floating through life. When we're not focused, our dreams seem more distant, impossible to achieve.

The other obstacle that stops us from becoming elite individuals is, simply, ourselves. How many times have you had an idea or an urge to do something out of the ordinary to elevate yourself in some way, but then a little voice in your head has said, "that's a stupid idea," or "no, you're not good enough for that." The reality is, that voice is the enemy. Fear is our enemy! These trepidations make us unmotivated to go on and become great. Then we stop believing in ourselves.

So how do we get tunnel vision toward becoming greater? What is it that will elevate us? Through all of the psychological noise, it is vitally important that we constantly remind ourselves of our goals. The noise may be present, but we still see our goals and dreams as clear as day. Many people around you will *not* understand your vision. They will not agree with what you're trying to do. The reason why they don't believe in you is because God gave you the vision for a reason. It's *yours,* and it's no one else's. That's why you have to work your butt off to make it manifest. Believing in yourself when nobody else will is crucial, because the psychological noise will never stop. If you cannot stay focused through the chaos that surrounds you, then it will be extremely hard for you to become great.

Essentially, that's what God wants from us; he wants us to be the best that we can be by using all of our talents that he has blessed us with.

Having gifts that differ according to the grace given to us, let us use them: if prophecy, in proportion to our faith; if service, in our serving, the one who teaches, in his teaching; the one who exhorts, in his exhortation, the one who contributes, in generosity; the one who leads, with zeal; the one who does act of mercy, with cheerfulness. - Romans 12:6-8

Peace Be Still

Living in a world of chaos can lead to frustration. Another method of quieting the psychological noise is meditation. Meditation can be associated with prayer because it can be seen as aligning yourself with God and the universe. The main objective of meditation is to literally quiet our busy minds. This can be done by simply finding a place that is comfortable, quiet, and away from any possible distractions.

Find a comfortable place to sit while making sure that your back is upright. You can also use music that is most soothing and relaxing. A good example would be the sound of soft classical music or the sounds of nature. Close your eyes and begin to inhale and exhale slowly. Try to silence all of the different thoughts that surface. This may take a while, since our minds are constantly racing, so be very patient (it usually takes between 25-40 minutes). Once you get to a point where your mind is silenced, and the frequent random thoughts subside, that's when you become at peace. When you're at peace with yourself, the outside world becomes almost irrelevant. All of your worries and disappointments fade. Clarity will fall upon you. The peace that is within you will help to guide you. The stillness of your mind will unleash an unexplainable joy while revealing your true identity as a human being. This stillness can be found at home, through nature, at your local park, or anywhere that promotes tranquility and placidity.

You should meditate as often as possible. It can be done in the morning, afternoon, evening, or whenever you have free time away from the hectic world. The peace, joy and clarity that you experience through meditation will help you "filter out the fog" that slows you from your goals and aspirations.

Tip #3 There's no Excuse for Excuses

"Excuses are tools of the incompetent used by the weak that build monuments that lead to nowhere. Those who use them seldom amount to anything." - Anonymous

"I do not believe in excuses. I believe in hard work as the prime solvent of life's problems." - James Cash Penney

If you know of any individuals who constantly make excuses for their circumstances, try your best to avoid them, or to enlighten them. Excuses are contagious. They're an attempt to make someone feel sorry for you. Once you start using them, it's hard to stop. Try not to make this a habit. It just makes us seem weak. That's how one can differentiate successful individuals from others. Successful people don't dwell in excuses. They make things happen regardless of the circumstances.

Excuses come in different forms. They can be related to emotions, for instance. Maybe you don't feel well, or someone made you angry that day. Nonetheless, it is important to use all negative energy in your favor. Many people cry and feel sorry for themselves, and some look for pity and grief from others, but successful individuals know how to transform negative energy and utilize it as motivation. We challenge you, the next time someone or something thing makes you mad, sad, or somewhere in between, to take a look at your vision. Choose one thing from your list, board, or document, and work on it, even if it is only for 5 minutes. We assure you that, after a few times, this habit will become second nature, and more importantly, it will keep you moving towards success.

Time is another driver of excuses. Those who fall under the will of excuses often blame it on time. Maybe you tell yourself you will get to it later in the week, or by the end of the month. Next thing you know, a year has passed and no progress has been made. To limit your excuses, get in the habit of doing things *now*. You can't get back the time of yesterday; once that time is gone, that day's opportunity is forever lost. The value of the present day should be cherished and utilized to the best of your ability.

Now is always the time. It can be an assignment, business venture, or a book you're writing. Do something that gets the ball rolling in that instant. We suggest writing down your excuse every time you think of one. Self-realization will be the key to addressing excuses and disowning them as you move forward.

When you find yourself making excuses for things that are detrimental to your success, immediately change your frame of thinking. A lot of times we make excuses to find a way out, or because we're flat-out lazy. Next time, face whatever excuse presents itself and talk to it. (Yes, talk to it!) Tell the excuse, "I'm not going to let you hold me back from my ultimate goal." Then train your mind to think that the only way past the task at hand is to accomplish it. Eliminate the option of finding a way out. While in college, the students at the business school had a saying: "No excuse is acceptable. No amount of effort is adequate until proven effective."

No more excuses. Let's make believers out of disbelievers.

Tip #4 Timing is Everything

"Lost time is never found again." - *Benjamin Franklin*

"Yesterday's the past, tomorrow's the future, but today is a gift. That's why it's called the present." - *Bill Keane*

We hate the phrase "time is money." We think its meaning is as far from the truth as it could be. Why? Because time is the most valuable resource that we can ever have. You can lose money and get it back, but you can *never* get back time. It's always limited. If there isn't anything that should motivate us to move diligently towards our goals, it should be that the clock is always ticking.

We can sometimes get distracted from our goals and our ambitions due to our surroundings, which, consequently, lead us to waste time. Social media is one of the most innovative and useful creations of late, and it has certainly changed the world. However, it can also serve as a large time consumer for individuals. According to CNBC and a Nielsen Social Media Report, Americans spent 121 billion minutes on social media sites in July 2012 alone. That's 388 minutes—or 6-1/2 hours—per person (if every person in the U.S. used social media). Altogether, that adds up to 230,060 years we spent staring into the screen! Television is another culprit. How much of our valuable time do we give to people on our television screens? The fact of the matter is that our time is steadily being wasted while we watch others live their dreams. Everybody has the same 24 hours, but some people just know how to make the best out of their time, which is why they achieve more.

Just think, while you're relaxing under the sun, or shooting the breeze, someone else may be working hard to take whatever spot you're striving for. Now don't get it confused, I'm not saying that there isn't time for rest and relaxation. However, that same rest and relaxation should be a portion of the fruit of your labor. For example, partying is something that many of us love. But the problem is that some of us party way too much. Partying should be a form of celebration for the hard work that has been done. Why should you be partying if you're failing classes in school? Or better yet, why should you be partying if you're funds are extremely low and you're in financial distress? What are you celebrating? The partying is always sweeter and has more meaning when you're celebrating your accomplishments.

We should always make sure that our actions are aligned with our future goals. Next time you're not doing much of anything, ask yourself, "what can I be doing right now to get myself closer to my goals?" or "what can I be doing to help prepare me for the next level?" Whether the results will come two months from the present, or two years, do something to prepare yourself for that day. Henry Hartman says, "Success always comes when preparation meets opportunity." Opportunities to be great only come every so often, so ask yourself, "will I be great, or will my opportunity pass me by because I wasn't prepared to answer its call?" Let's not take that chance.

Tony Gaskins, a world-renowned life coach, made a point that will stick with us forever. He came up with an acronym that encompasses what using our time wisely really means: S.W.A.G. Stop Watching and Grind.

Stop watching others live their dreams and get to work on making yours a reality.

Tip #5 Average is Boring

"Average is the worst, most disgusting word in the English language. Nothing meaningful or worthwhile ever came from that word." - Portia de Rossi

"I've never viewed myself as particularly talented. I've viewed myself as slightly above average in talent. Where I excel is with a ridiculous, sickening work ethic. While the other guy's sleeping, I'm working. While the other guy's eating, I'm working. While the other guy's making love, I mean, I'm making love, too, but I'm working really hard at it!" - *Will Smith*

During childhood, everyone has dreams, and some even have goals that they want to accomplish. When asked what we want to be when we grow up, we reply with something farfetched like an astronaut, a scientist, a billionaire, or the president. This sort of thinking is far from average, but at the time seems reachable and easy to attain. As we grow older and learn more, however, something happens, and we become more conscious of our surroundings. Where did that extreme dream-chasing, above-average, unrealistic mindset we were all born with go? After childhood, most start to become more "realistic," and in turn they develop average thinking. Their dreams are scaled back; they no longer desire to be a billionaire, or an astronaut, and they become perfectly fine with working an average job with an average salary, which they approach with a below-average morale. Subsequently, they then surround themselves with average friends and, consequently, live out an average life until death.

    The aforementioned scenario is why Tip #5 advises you all to stay away from being *average*. In fact, we urge you to eliminate this word from your vocabulary along with *can't*, *maybe*, *impossible*, and *unrealistic*. As we all have seen firsthand, the success of others has proven over and again that these words only hinder positive movement. No matter how old you are when someone asks what you want out of life, think of the most realistic answer and completely surpass it! When more people believe that they will become billionaires, CEO's, entrepreneurs, activists, fashion gurus, and more, a society made up of above-average occupants will present itself. According to the Washington Post, there are nearly 8 million millionaires in the U.S alone. It is possible, and it is being done every day. If *millions* of individuals are making their financial goals a reality, there is no reason why we shouldn't set the bar high and plan to make each of our dreams come true as well.

You can scream your goals and ambitions from the rooftop and dare someone to doubt them. Or you can move in silence, showing people what you're capable of rather than telling them. No matter what route you choose, the message is the same: average is boring! Many individuals constantly create *what could've been* or *what should've been* scenarios in their heads to allow themselves to spend more time fantasizing about the lives of others rather than creating a life of their own. They live full of regret, never reaching their full potential and never knowing what they were truly capable of. If you train yourself to think average, and use the horrid words like "can't," "impossible," or "unrealistic," you limit your thinking and become trapped in a box of mediocrity.

Tip #6 Turn Lemons into Lemon Meringue Pie

"Stop expecting life to give you lemons, and if it does, get excited, they may be just the ingredients you need for your personal story of success." - A.D. Williams

"Failure is the condiment that gives success its flavor." - Truman Capote

Many are familiar with the phrase, "Shoot for the moon. Even if you miss, you will land among the stars" (Norman Vincent Peale, Les Brown). This phrase sells the idea that if you set your goals high enough, even falling short of them will be an accomplishment. With this thought in mind, maybe we can change your perception of what failure entails. The end result of such failures, after we learn from them, represent the true masterpiece: a smudge that became the first brush stroke of a magnificent painting.

Sour to Sweet

Have you ever had lemon meringue pie?! It's delicious! Even if you haven't tried it, or if you've tried it but didn't like it, you get the point. You've probably heard the saying, "When life hands you lemons, make lemonade." We have nothing against the saying, but we just think lemon meringue pie is even better. Once you add different ingredients, like sugar, flour, and butter, it turns out to be a fluffy, sweet dessert. The sugar can represent your true supporters that believe in you and your abilities. The flour may represent your resiliency, and your ability to keep your composure throughout the tough times. The butter may be seen as your ambition, the deep desire to win. Combine all of your ingredients with your sour lemons to create something magical and delicious.

We all know life can be difficult. Hardships, obstacles, and tragedies all come in different forms. Sometimes things happen that we can control, and sometimes things happen that are out of our hands. From being labeled a failure, to facing rejection and disappointment, to suffering the loss of someone close to us, any number of things can make our lives more difficult than it already is. These issues will never cease. So what is the one thing that we can do?

You got it: turn lemons into lemon meringue pie.

We have to learn to turn something so sour into something sweet and delicious. If something doesn't necessarily go our way, we should look at it as feedback rather than thinking that all is lost. Although it may be difficult, this trait is a must-have for successful people. Make it a habit to try and turn darkness into light regardless of the situation at hand. Whatever negative energy burdens you, learn how to turn that same energy into something positive. Negative situations turned positive make for the best success stories. Thankfully, a guy named Walt turned lemons into lemon meringue pie after being fired from his newspaper job when they told him that he "lacked imagination and had no new ideas." If Walt would've let his firing discourage him from being great, then we wouldn't have Walt Disney World. Through these tough times, you will build character, resilience, and a certain level of confidence you never would have gained had you continued to lay dormant while basking in misery. Frustration, anger, sadness, or any other emotion you feel through these times won't make the situation any better. But learning to channel that energy and emotion into forward action most definitely will.

    Think about it, if we train ourselves to turn any negative situation into something positive, who or what can really hurt us?

Tip #7 Love What You Do, and Do What You Love

"The biggest mistake that you can make is to believe that you are working for somebody else...The driving force of a career must come from the individual. Remember: Jobs are owned by the company, you own your career!" – Earl Nightingale

"Passion will move men beyond themselves, beyond their shortcomings, beyond their failures." – Joseph Campbell

Sometimes we have the tendency to ignore our talents, our passions, and whatever makes us happy. Sometimes we neglect these things because they are not profitable. Others times we neglect them because of what others might think. Regardless of the reasoning, it's extremely important to do what you love and love what you do. Again, your ideas and talents were not given to you by accident. God gave them to you so that you could share them with the world. We were all put on this earth to serve others in some capacity. The world needs your services!

What is an activity that you both love, and wouldn't mind doing for free? Whichever activity chosen is what you ultimately should be doing. What if J.K Rowling decided not to continue writing because she didn't see the money coming in right away? Then we wouldn't have Harry Potter. If Steve Jobs did not live and breathe for Apple, we wouldn't have the iPhone. When passion is present in your work, something magical happens. The individuals whom we deem as great, or powerful, each went through major challenges and burdens in life which we all (at some time or another) experience. Each respectively endured letdowns, but each decided that temporary failure was only feedback, and continued on. Regardless of your skill-set, finances, or other circumstances, your passion has the ability to manifest greatness.

As you pursue success, do not get sucked into the idea of chasing money or jobs. You will find that following money alone can lead to temporary satisfaction, resulting in a short-term victory. Passion is alive in all of us. And with preparation, that passion has the power to equip even those who are lacking in every other category with the tools needed to survive the journey to success. Before you explore the internet or dive into books, you must look within. The desire and need to succeed must be self-realized and can only be done with sufficient effort. Once this love is found, you will surely see your work and efforts multiply.

It is truly beautiful to see how passion can drive one through time and towards achievement. The key is to do what you love. Some individuals' lives consist of working at a job they despise for their entire life while saving for retirement, retiring, then planning to enjoy life as retired elderly citizens. Society has trained some of us to think this way. When you truly love what you do, work doesn't necessarily feel like work. Essentially, you and work will become harmonious, and you will approach it with certain ardor every day.

Tip #8 Fear is Fictional

"There is only one thing that makes a dream impossible to achieve: the fear of failure." – Paulo Coelho

"Only Thing We Have to Fear Is Fear Itself."- Franklin D. Roosevelt

Fear can be broken down into an acronym.

False. Evidence. Appearing. Real.

Actual fear is created only in our heads. Fear is nothing more than false fantasies appearing to deceive us; they stop us in our tracks and prevent us from moving forward. Our fear places us in an invisible prison. It's OK to recognize the fear, but it's not OK to let fear hinder you from taking the necessary steps to achieve greatness. The key is to face your fear directly and walk by faith. Once you've overcome fear, that's when the magic can happen. Fear is often the only thing that separates us from achieving greatness. Be fearless, and never be afraid to venture out into the unknown. It is easy to stay comfortable and in the confines of our personal bubble, but sometimes it will take more. Realizing what you are destined for and achieving success will take some risks and- fortitude. No worries! We are constantly reminded that high risks equal high rewards.

Think of the shepherd boy from Paulo Coelho's *The Alchemist*. This book tells a story of a young Andalusian shepherd boy who was courageous enough to follow his dreams, literally. The young boy suffers from a recurring dream urging him to seek treasure that lies at the Egyptian Pyramids. The boy left his home and embarked on a magnificent journey that, in the end, led him to the treasure. What is remarkable about the story is that the treasure was not found at the pyramids, but at the very place in which his dreams began.

If you can step out of your comfort zone and not fear the journey, all the success in the world can be yours. We learn a valuable lesson from the young shepherd boy. We all have dreams that persist, but few of us have the guts to travel into the unknown to make them a reality. The road to success is the one less traveled. Learn from the young shepherd in your times of discomfort. Never let fear sign your checks and determine your destiny. In every difficult situation, we decide on what emotion we will choose: faith or fear. If we choose fear, then we must not believe in God's omnipotent power. If we choose faith, we must believe that He is with us every step of the way.

So have faith and allow your dreams and visions to pull you out into the world for the ultimate adventure.

Tip #9 Believe in Yourself

"Whether you think you can or think you can't — you are right." - Henry Ford

"Confidence is going after Moby Dick in a rowboat and taking the tartar sauce with you." - Zig Ziglar

This is probably the most important tip of all: self-belief. When striving for our goals, it's very easy for us to become unmotivated. We may have an idea of who or what we want to be or where we want to go, but sometimes our lack of confidence gets in the way. It is extremely important to look within to find God within you. Loving yourself unconditionally is an essential part of confidence. Love yourself despite all of your faults. Have faith in both your ideas and in the person you want to become.

In *Think and Grow Rich*, Napoleon Hill writes, "Ideas are intangible forces, but they have more power than the physical brains that give birth to them. They have the power to live on, after the brain that creates them has returned to dust." Once one can realize that most of the things around us, from our cell phones, to our automobiles, to the restaurants at which we stuff our faces, were once merely an idea that sat quietly in someone's brain, then one can understand the true power of our thoughts. In other words, the ideas that are partnered with hard work and *action* can literally change the world and live on forever. Even though Thomas Alva Edison has passed on, the insane idea that he once had of an electric light has continued to flow through time, and now the world is lit by electric power. Our thoughts and ideas can be manifested into their physical equivalents. That's why it's imperative for us to walk upright, and to have unmatched confidence at all times.

Think of yourself as your favorite super-hero. Once you're able to look within, to find your true worth as a human being, nothing or no one can muddle your confidence. You have to have faith in yourself when no one else believes in you. People criticized Orville and Wilbur Wright when they revealed what they were working on. Their dreams were too big for others to understand. But that didn't stop the Wright brothers from creating the first airplane. The seemingly impossible idea of metal flying across the skies with people inside is very much alive today.

An equally important guideline is to not let your surroundings determine your net worth. Society is known for labeling us. A failing test grade doesn't mean that you're incompetent. Not receiving the job offer that you wanted doesn't mean that you're not good enough to perform in that capacity. Our true self-worth and potential cannot be quantified or measured: because God is our source and he has infinite power. So remember, never let anyone or anything deter you from realizing your truth worth.

Let us revisit John's situation from the introduction. After much thought, John finally made the decision to follow his dreams as a movie producer. The decision was very difficult at first but he mustered up enough courage to start his journey.

After years of working diligently, facing obstacles, believing in himself, and focusing on his goals, he found himself on the set of a film with clipboard in hand, special lighting, cameras everywhere, yelling at his actors to get in place. "This is NOT how I envisioned this scene!" shouted John. After hearing his statement, John chuckled inside. He thought that the statement was ironic due to the fact that it was EXACTLY how he had envisioned this moment years ago, as he sat miserably in his cubicle at a data processing company. But back then it was it was only a dream.

It should be no secret by now that the real world and what you get out of it comes from your actions and thoughts. Your ability to dream big, to refine those dreams over time, and to overcome fear will determine your destiny. The valuable tips listed above will be futile without good-faith effort and a deep-rooted desire for success that can only come from within. To all creative individuals, please do us all a favor and release your work into to the world,

because it is your art of self-expression that has shaped and molded this world since its existence.
Now is the time!

*Stay **Young** in spirit, **Fly** above the norm, and be **Foolish** enough to believe that you can change the world.*

Best of luck to you as you set out to conquer all your dreams and aspirations!

With Love,
Thank you for your time and support. Please leave us a review and tell us what you think on Amazon! Or you can email us @ youngflyandfoolish@gmail.com.

Made in the USA
Middletown, DE
30 August 2017